30 2-INGREDIENT RECIPES AND HELPFUL HINTS FOR THE BUSY HOMEMAKER

SUSIE KINSLOW ADAMS

ISBN: 1978433069
ISBN-13: 978-1978433069

Table of Contents

Have you decided to prepare healthier meals? Perhaps you have even restocked cabinets with more whole grains, fresh vegetables and fruits and less bakery and sweet snacks. We know…most of our well-intentioned changes fail to last over a few weeks.

Use these recipes to regularly plan small surprise treats for your family. Purchase a few needed ingredients and store them in a safe place. Then you will be ready to surprise family and friends. The good thing is you won't have tons of leftovers and be tempted to get back into the snack habit.

Easy preparation, no mess, and smaller quantities (no leftovers tempting you all week) make these quick snack and simple bakery hints a snap. Included are some helpful substitutions and hints to simplify your valuable kitchen time.

-Susie

2-INGREDIENT DESSERTS, SNACKS AND MORE

Cookies n Cream Oreo Bark

(A 20-minute sweet simple dessert)

Ingredients:

1. 10 oz. white chocolate chips
2. 15 regular size Oreos, chopped (plus 3)

Directions:

Line an 8×8 pan with wax paper

Heat chocolate, and then cool 5 minutes

Chop 15 Oreos and stir into chocolate

Pour into pan

Sprinkle remaining three crumbled Oreos on top

Chill 10 minutes and break into pieces.

Strawberry Fudge

...for "I just have to have something NOW"

Ingredients:

1. 12 oz. bag white chocolate chips
2. 16 oz. bag of strawberry frosting

Directions:

Soften white chocolate chips and strawberry frosting in microwave.

Mix well, refrigerate in 9x9 pan to set.

Cut in squares to serve.

For an added treat, top with fresh strawberries.

Peanut Butter Fudge

Ingredients:

1. One 15 oz. jar peanut butter (smooth or crunchy)
2. One container of vanilla or cream cheese cake frosting OR 1 pound white almond bark.

*For extra goodness, use a can of chocolate cake frosting or chocolate almond bark.

Directions:

Mix well, refrigerate in 9x9 pan to set.

Cut in squares to serve.

 # Another Yummy Fudge Recipe

Ingredients:
1. 3 cups of chocolate chips
2. 1 can sweetened condensed milk

Directions:

Heat chocolate chips and 1 can sweetened condensed milk until chips melt.

Pour onto greased 8x8 inch pan

Refrigerate, cut into pieces.

**Optional - nuts may be added to recipe if desired.

 # Peanut Butter Fudge Recipe

Ingredients:
1. 3/4 cup creamy peanut butter
2. 3 ½ cups (2 packages) butterscotch morsels

Directions:

Combine 3/4 cup creamy peanut butter and 3 ½ cups (2 packages) butterscotch morsels

Melt together in microwave, stirring every 30 seconds.

Pour into buttered 8x8 pan

Cool 4 hours, cut in pieces and enjoy!

Simple, Nutritious Hot Chocolate

Ingredients:

1. 4 cups whole milk
2. ½ cup Nutella

<u>Directions:</u>

Warm 4 cups whole milk

Add ½ cup Nutella

Mix well and serve hot.

Healthy, Flourless Apple Pie

Ingredients:

1. 4 ½ pounds apples
2. 2 ¼ pounds millet

<u>Directions:</u>

Peel and grate 4 ½ pounds apples

Mix in 2 ¼ pounds millet

Bake in buttered 9×13 pan 90 minutes at 200 degrees.

Cool before serving.

Flavorful Ranch Biscuits

Ingredients:

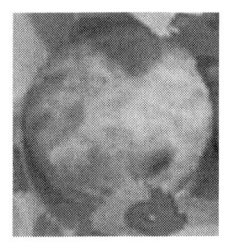

1. 2 ¼ cups biscuit mix
2. 2/3 cup Ranch dressing

Directions:

Thoroughly mix 2 ¼ cups biscuit mix and 2/3 cup Ranch dressing.

Shape into biscuits

Bake at 450 for 10 minutes.

Quick Pizza Dough

Ingredients:

1. 1 ½ cups self-rising flour
2. 1 cup Greek yogurt

Directions:

Combine the yogurt and 1 cup of flour in a bowl.

Mix until combined.

Add flour until dough doesn't stick to your hands.

Knead dough 5-8 minutes until smooth, about 5-8 minutes, adding flour as needed.

Roll out the dough; add toppings.

Bake 450 degree for 10-12 minutes.

**Makes 2 medium pizza crusts.

10 2-Ingredient Coconut Macaroons

Ingredients:

1. 1 package of coconut flakes
2. 1 can of sweetened condensed milk

Directions:

Combine the coconut and sweetened condensed milk. Mixture should be very sticky.

Turn on the broiler.

Drop in balls on cookie sheet

Broil a few minutes until brown. Watch carefully that they do not burn.

Dip in chocolate if preferred.

11 Banana Oatmeal Cookies

Ingredients:

1. 2 ripe bananas (defrost frozen bananas if you have them)
2. 1 cup quick oats

Directions:

Mash and measure bananas to equal one cup.

Mix ingredients together (it's okay if there are small chunks of banana).

Bake 350 degrees for 15 minutes on a GREASED cookie sheet.

If mix is too runny, cookies will flatten when baked. Add more oatmeal.

Add a few more ingredients for these cookies:

Brown Sugar-Cinnamon Raisin Cookies
Add 2 tbsp. raisins, ½ tsp. cinnamon, and 1 tsp. brown sugar to the batter.

Almond Butter-Chocolate Chip Cookies
Add 2 tbsp. mini chocolate chips and 2 tbsp. almond butter (or peanut butter) to the batter.

 **12**   **Six Mini Banana Pancakes (no flour)**

Ingredients:
1. 1 banana
2. 2 eggs

Directions:

Using a fork, mash one banana

Add two eggs and whisk together

Pour batter onto lightly oiled fry pan.

Top with syrup or chocolate syrup or bananas.

**Add cinnamon, vanilla, or chocolate chips for variety.

13 2-Ingredient Pumpkin Muffins Recipe

Ingredients:

1. 1 cake mix (any flavor works, but chocolate is a favorite!)
2. 1 can pumpkin or 2 cups mashed cooked pumpkin

Directions:

Combine cake mix and pumpkin
Beat until smooth. (It will be really thick)

Use ice cream scoop to put batter into muffin cups or tins.

Bake at 350 degrees for 20 minutes.

Serve hot with butter.

VARIATIONS:

**Vary recipe with spice cake mix or add chips: chocolate, white, peanut butter, or butterscotch.

*Makes 24 from one box of mix.

MEATS AND MAIN DISHES

14 **Perk up an Ordinary Pot Roast**

Ingredients:

1. 3 lbs. round steak or beef chuck roast
2. 1 envelope dry brown gravy mix.

Directions:

Place 3 lbs. round steak or beef chuck roast on heavy aluminum foil.

Sprinkle with 1 envelope brown gravy mix.

Wrap tightly, roast in pan at 300 degrees for 3 hours.

Make a pan sauce with the juices or pour over meat.

15 Simple 2-Ingredient Juicy Chicken

Ingredients:

1. 6 skinless, boneless chicken breast halves
2. 16 ounce bottle Italian-style salad dressing

Directions:

Marinate overnight.
Bake on lightly greased pan for 1 hour at 350 degrees.

 **16 Add Zest to Plain Fish:**

Ingredients:

1. 1 lb. tilapia fillets
2. 14.5 oz. can stewed tomatoes

Directions:

Heat tomatoes in large skillet

Add tilapia and spoon tomatoes over tilapia to coat

Cover skillet and simmer until fish flakes easily, about 10 minutes.

 **17 Succulent Pot Roast**

Ingredients:

1. 3 lbs. round steak or beef chuck roast
2. 1 envelope dry onion soup mix

Directions:

Place meat on a 18x12" sheet of heavy duty aluminum foil

Sprinkle dry soup mix over meat.

NOTE:
For one-dish meal, unwrap meat after 2 hours; add small red potatoes, baby carrots, whole mushrooms, peppers, and onions. Re-wrap and bake another hour or until vegetables are tender.

Wrap tightly in foil, using double folds.

Roast in roasting pan 3 hours at 300 degrees or until the meat is very tender.

Unwrap the meat and place on a serving platter.

Pour the juices over the meat and serve, or make a pan sauce with the juices.

18   Salsa Crockpot Chicken

Ingredients:

1.   3 pounds boneless, skinless chicken thighs
2.   1 (16-oz) jar peach salsa.

Directions:

Combine chicken thighs and salsa in a 3 to 4 quart crockpot. You can layer the thighs or cube the chicken and mix with salsa.

Cover and cook on low for 6-8 hours, until the chicken is tender and thoroughly cooked.

Leave lid off and cook on high for 30-45 minutes to thicken, or add 2 tablespoons cornstarch mixed with ¼ cup of water; cover and cook 20-30 minutes longer on low.

19   3-Ingredient Crescent Dogs

Ingredients:

1.   8 hot dogs
2.   4 slices American cheese cut into 6 strips
3.   1 8-oz. can crescent dinner rolls.

Directions:

Slit hot dogs to within ½ inch of ends
Insert strips of cheese into each slit
Wrap with crescent dinner roll triangle.
Bake on ungreased cookie sheet, cheese side up for 12-15 minutes at 375F until golden brown.

USEFUL HINTS AND TIME SAVERS

20

Ham Marinade

Ingredients:

1. 2 parts ginger ale
2. 1 part mustard

Directions:

Mix together and use as a marinade on ham. This keeps the meat moist and tasty.

Make Foods Chocolate-ier!

To make foods made with chocolate more chocolate-ier. Use HOT water instead of cold to mix cocoa to develop its flavor. This wakes up the flavor, much like brewing coffee beans does to coffee.

Make Your Own Self-Rising Flour

Make self-rising flour from regular flour by adding 1 ½ tsp. Baking powder and ¾ tsp. salt to 1½ cups flour.

Fresh Spices

For healthier, better flavor meals, make sure your spices are not outdated. Larger jars are not necessarily cheaper if you don't use them before they get old and lose flavor.

Refresh Fresh Herbs

Cooking with fresh herbs adds flavor and nutrition. If you have wilted herbs not stored properly, you can refresh them by giving them an ice-water bath for about an hour. Then dry them and store properly: cut stems off and store on paper towel in zip lock bag or airtight container.

SIMPLE TIPS

MAKE BOXED CAKES BETTER

25   Add Extra Moistness to a Cake

For extra moistness, add two extra egg yolks –which means more fat—but adds the density and moisture of a bakery cake!

26   Add Extra Flavor to a Cake

When your box mix calls for liquid, add milk and not water. The milk adds density, fat, and extra flavor to your mix.

Add more Flavor

When using only egg whites and not yolks, add one extra tablespoon of butter for each removed egg yolk. Not adding the yolks to the cake removes the fat; the butter replaces it and adds flavor.

Freshen the Taste of Boxed Cake Mix

To freshen up boxed cake mixes, add a dash of vanilla extract. Add ½ teaspoon of vanilla extract for better flavor as box mixes tend to lose flavor as they sit on store shelves.

Add Richness to Cake

For all cake mixes, use melted butter instead of oil. Both add fat but butter adds a richness and depth of flavor that most boxed cakes are missing.

Keep Cake from Spilling Over Edge

Sprinkle the top of your cake with sugar before baking. This gives a sweet, crunchy texture and also prevents the cake from rising too much while it bakes.

About the Author

Susie Kinslow Adams

Susie Kinslow Adams is a wife, mother, and grandmother whose earliest memories are of caring for grandparents and offering hugs and hope to shy or struggling classmates. Her work alongside her husband in ministry has provided years of experience with groups and individuals from children to senior adults. Susie is a gifted author, writer, speaker, and storyteller.

Susie's free newsletter, *Caring from the Heart*, gives practical tips and help for caregivers as well as real hope for daily living. She and her husband, Russell, live in Buffalo, Missouri.

See more stories of hope and encouraging words at
www.susiekinslowadams.com

Made in the USA
Monee, IL
02 July 2024

60863450R00015